THE SOUND
OF

D1515807

Also by Harold Klemp

Animals Are Soul Too!
The Art of Spiritual Dreaming
Autobiography of a Modern
  Prophet
The Call of Soul
A Cosmic Sea of Words: The
  ECKANKAR Lexicon
ECKANKAR's Spiritual
  Experiences Guidebook
ECK Masters and You: An
  Illustrated Guide
ECK Wisdom Temples, Spiritual
  Cities, & Guides: A Brief History
Is Life a Random Walk?
A Modern Prophet Answers Your
  Key Questions about Life, Books
  1 and 2
Past Lives, Dreams, and Soul Travel
The Spiritual Exercises of ECK
The Spiritual Laws of Life
Those Wonderful ECK Masters
Youth Ask a Modern Prophet about
  Life, Love, and God

The Mahanta Transcripts Series

Journey of Soul, Book 1
How to Find God, Book 2
The Secret Teachings, Book 3
The Golden Heart, Book 4
Cloak of Consciousness, Book 5
Unlocking Your Sacred Puzzle Box,
  Book 6
The Eternal Dreamer, Book 7
The Dream Master, Book 8
We Come as Eagles, Book 9
The Drumbeat of Time, Book 10
What Is Spiritual Freedom? Book 11
How the Inner Master Works,
  Book 12
The Slow Burning Love of God,
  Book 13

The Secret of Love, Book 14
Our Spiritual Wake-Up Calls,
  Book 15
How to Survive Spiritually in Our
  Times, Book 16
The Road to Spiritual Freedom,
  Book 17

The Immortality of Soul Series

The Awakened Heart
The Awakening Soul
HU, the Most Beautiful Prayer
The Language of Soul
Love—The Keystone of Life
The Loving Heart
The Spiritual Life
Touching the Face of God
Truth Has No Secrets

ECK Wisdom Series

ECK Wisdom on Conquering Fear
ECK Wisdom on Dreams
ECK Wisdom on Inner Guidance
ECK Wisdom on Karma and
  Reincarnation
ECK Wisdom on Life after Death
ECK Wisdom on Solving Problems

Spiritual Wisdom Series

Spiritual Wisdom on Health and
  Healing
Spiritual Wisdom on Prayer,
  Meditation, and Contemplation
Spiritual Wisdom on
  Relationships

Stories to Help You See God in Your Life

The Book of ECK Parables, Volumes
  1, 2, and 3
Stories to Help You See God in Your
  Life, ECK Parables, Book 4

This book has been authored by and published under
the supervision of the Mahanta, the Living ECK Master,
Sri Harold Klemp. It is the Word of ECK.

THE SOUND

OF SOUL

HAROLD KLEMP

ECKANKAR
Minneapolis
www.Eckankar.org

The Sound of Soul

Printed in USA

ISBN: 978-1-57043-455-6

Edited by Patrick Carroll, Joan Klemp, and Anthony Moore

Photo of Sri Harold Klemp (pages viii and 81) by Art Galbraith

Second printing—2018

Library of Congress Cataloging-in-Publication Data

Names: Klemp, Harold, author.
Title: The sound of soul / Harold Klemp.
Description: Minneapolis : Eckankar, 2017.
Identifiers: LCCN 2017043519 | ISBN 9781570434556 (pbk. : alk. paper)
Subjects: LCSH: Eckankar (Organization) | Spiritual life--Eckankar (Organization)
Classification: LCC BP605.E3 K573 2017 | DDC 299/.93--dc23
LC record available at https://lccn.loc.gov/2017043519

♾ This paper meets the requirements of ANSI/NISO Z39.48-1992 (Permanence of Paper).

Table of Contents

A Higher Perspective • Letting God Speak • The Silver Lining

Sri Harold Klemp
The Mahanta, the Living ECK Master

Introduction

Welcome to the worlds of HU, an ancient, universal name for God. This sacred word can spiritually uplift people of any religion, culture, or walk of life. It is freely given—a gift beyond measure.

HU is the Sound behind all sounds, woven into the language of life.

It is the wind in the leaves, falling rain, thunder of jets, singing of birds, the awful rumble of a tornado. Its sound is heard in laughter, weeping, the din of city traffic, ocean waves, and the quiet rippling of a mountain stream. It is a word people anywhere can use to address the Originator of Life.

In time you may come to know it as the audible whisper of God's love stirring in your very atoms. A proof that Soul exists because God loves It.

The ancient brotherhood of ECK Adepts has known of it for centuries. They chose the present age to bring knowledge of it to the modern world. To you—today. Sing it from your heart, and there will be infinite ways to benefit from its blessings.

Love opens you to its guidance, peace, healing of body, mind, and spirit, and to the highest form of creativity.

And whom do you love?

God, the Creator, Divine Intelligence, the Holy Spirit, the ECK, the Life Force, the All in All, the One. Or just love your family, pets, your neighbor as yourself, the flowers you watered today. Love is love.

And you are that. HU is the Sound of Soul.

HU will prepare you to accept the full love of God in this lifetime. Begin today. Find a quiet spot, shut your eyes, and let love for something dear to you enter your heart. Sing *HU* gently aloud, then silently for ten to twenty minutes. Look and listen for the love that returns to you. This is a law of the universe.

Love returns love.

So sing *HU*, a love song to God, every day.

$\mathcal{L}$OVE

HU is a carrier of love
between Soul and God

The Sound of Life

What is HU?

It is a very holy name for God. In it are contained all sounds.

When you sing *HU*, know that this is one of the most sacred names for God. Sing it with love and with reverence. Look for the Light, listen for the Sound.

People singing softly to each other, the song is of the HU. People laughing, the laughter is of the HU. And even when there are people crying, the crying is of the HU.

The falling rain, its sound is of the HU. And the birds, and the wind.

These are all of the sound of HU.

The Reason for Living

So what is the reason for living?

Life is God's blessing to each Soul—you—
to learn how to give and receive love. That's
what's going on behind the scenes in this
great laboratory of life.

The secret of all time is that we are each to
be a steward of divine love.

Sing *HU*, and the blessings of love will
find you.

The Heart of God

The quickest way to put your state of con-
sciousness in the heart of God is to sing *HU*.
Just sing *HU* to yourself a few times with love.
You'll notice that something changes.

A Carrier of Love

*I*n most spiritual traditions, sound plays a part in uplifting the individual.

Religions such as Christianity, Judaism, and Buddhism have made use of sound in the form of hymns, chants, and prayers to help open the heart and go beyond intellectual knowledge. Muslims, Sufis, and Hindus chant or sing the holy names of God in their monasteries and temples around the world.

We are involved with the uplifting nature of sound and music every day.

Look at the positive feelings inspired by songs with personal meaning for us. Just hearing a familiar melody opens us again to another time and place.

And consider that our mother's heartbeat is one of the first sounds we experience in this world; then comes her voice. When she sings a lullaby, it's a carrier for love to her child.

In a similar way, HU is a carrier of love between you and God.

What Is Soul?

Soul? What is Soul? You *are* Soul!

Soul is a divine part of God. All that remains is for you to recognize yourself. And to recognize yourself as a divine part of God, you must first—and more than anything else—recognize every living thing also as this part of God. We are in this Ocean of Love and Mercy.

If there is nothing else than love in life, there is more than enough for all. So take this love that dwells in you and give it to the world.

Respect and Love

When the old teachers say, "Love your neighbor as yourself," you've got to start with respect for yourself before you can have respect and love for anything or anyone else. And one of the best ways to do this is to sing *HU*, the most beautiful prayer.

The nondirected prayer of the ECKist is the same as the one in Christianity: "Not my will, but Thine be done." In ECK, we say, "May the blessings be."

Doorway of Love

*L*ove is the doorway to spiritual freedom. And the Light and Sound of God opens that doorway of love. You must go through this doorway. You must have the love of God transform your life to realize the gift of spiritual freedom.

The song of HU will bring you that love. The song of HU can bring you that gift.

The Nature of Love

*D*ivine love has no conditions—it simply loves. God loves, but not because we deserve it or have earned it. The reason is simply that God is love, therefore God loves. We are Soul, God's creation, and It loves us because that is Its nature.

HU can be sung by anyone of any religion. It isn't meant to change your religion. HU will enhance it.

The Eternal Force

*W*hoever wants to unfold into a better spiritual person must always keep the name of God upon his lips and in his heart.

The most ancient and holy name of all for God is HU. Sing this word often. Sung silently or aloud, it will stir the eternal force of divine love within your heart.

Filled with Love

*I*f people would trust their heart and know that if they love God and open their heart—if they love God through loving their neighbor— they would find that God brings help and protection to them in ways that most people don't know.

The way to do that is to sing *HU* to yourself. You just sing this very quietly to yourself or inwardly. You may see the Light of God; it can be a blue light, a white light, a yellow light, or a green light. You can see it many different ways. Or you may hear the sound of tinkling bells, a flute, a full orchestra, or something as simple as a sigh.

But you will be filled with love.

Sing *HU*, and this may help you open your heart to God's love. Then you will find the miracles happening in your life too.

God's Sweet Love

Consciously open your heart to God's love, which is always and forever flowing out to you like a quiet mountain stream.

It's easy to do.

Sing *HU*, and, in your mind and heart, watch this quiet stream of God's love flow gently into your heart and being.

HU opens your heart to God. It opens you to God's sweet love.

TRUTH AND WISDOM

Sing *HU*, and you will have
the secret of truth in your heart

Show Me Truth

So when you ask the Creator, "Show me truth," be ready to receive it. You have to ask with a true and open heart.

Behind everything you do is the life pulse of the Holy Spirit, the Voice of God. The Voice of God speaks to us as the Light and Sound. This is what fills one with divine love.

Sing the word *HU*, a love song to God, and you will be opened up to divine love. Love will lead you to truth.

Holy Ground

*L*earn to go inside yourself, because this is the source of all truth. There are a lot of holy temples out here, but the most sacred of all is the temple inside you, because this is where you meet with the Holy Spirit.

How do you meet with the Holy Spirit?

If you're in Christianity, you pray. You come to the holy temple, to the holy of holies, through prayer. You meet on holy ground with your God. If you're a member of any other religion, you have a means of going to that holy of holies, whether it's meditation or contemplation or prayer.

Go to the holy of holies. It's the temple inside you. This is the place where all truth comes from. Before there were words, before there was a written Bible, there was the Word in the heart of mankind.

This is the temple. Go there.

Higher Direction

*W*hen you sing *HU*, this name for God, you're saying, "I open myself to the will of God. Not as I will, but as Thou wilt." You look to some direction higher than yourself.

Listening

*A*s you sing *HU*, you're simply saying, "Thy will be done."

We don't try to tell God what to do. We listen to hear what God's Voice is saying to us.

Destiny

Soul comes into the world to accomplish an assortment of tasks; these assignments, taken as a whole, make up Its destiny.

To set the tone for Its mission, Soul may come into either a healthy body or a sickly one; into comfortable means or poverty; with great intellect or a simple mind; with the favored color of skin for that era or not; once a male, again a female.

Destiny can be thought of as the equipment, talents, or gifts which a person brings to this life. It remains for each to use them wisely.

Yet once an individual begins to live in accord with the divine will, he will see his outer life run in new directions. A whole new chapter is begun as a page is turned in the Book of Life. Whatever is expected when one begins an earnest practice of the spiritual exercises, it is certain that the love of the

(continued)

Sound Current is smoldering in the center of the spirit.

Live the song of HU, and surrender your heart to its ways. Your life will never be the same.

A Greater Vision

You are starting as a limited human being set down in a world of plenty.

There is no limitation except for the limitations you have made for yourself. These limitations are very real.

One way to begin coming into a greater vision of life is to sing *HU* when you need help. You say, "I've made my plan. I'm now asking for God's help." Then as you work toward your plan, remember to sing *HU*.

An Edge for Health

*H*U, the secret name of God, opens you as a channel for the greater healing of Divine Spirit.

Every thought, word, or deed either purifies or pollutes the body. This is very important, very powerful, because it deals with your state of consciousness.

If, at some point, you need an edge for health or for peace of mind, look to what's coming into your world. Look to your form of music, or your form of news. Be aware of whatever ways you let the external world into your internal world.

What's coming in is going to go back out. Then it rebounds like an echo and returns to you. It strengthens and grows to have a very strong influence in your life. This influence can be for either beneficial things or harmful things. So the choice is yours.

Every thought, word, or deed either purifies or pollutes your body.

(continued)

22

The HU song is a purifier. It will uplift and strengthen you in wisdom and awareness.

The Secret Part

You can get to the most secret part of yourself through contemplation, through the Spiritual Exercises of ECK, through the sacred sound of HU. Contemplation is a conversation with the most secret, most genuine, and most mysterious part of yourself.

Sing *HU*, and listen with love.

For Truth

*T*he word *HU* will spiritualize you. It's an ancient name for God. Sing *HU* on the way to work, for instance, and you will find that you have a different way of looking at the people around you and at the work you do.

Just sing *HU* every day. Take it to heart, and then go about your daily life.

Wherever you are, do the things that are necessary: bring home the groceries, sweep the floor. Do these things, and someday you will find that you have the secret of truth in your hand. You will have the secret of truth in your heart.

HU can show you truth.

Your Mission

I would encourage you to be eagles in Spirit, to recognize your heritage as a spiritual being able to rise at will into the higher planes of God. When you live with the song of HU in your heart, you are letting the highest principle in life direct you to the experiences you need.

The ultimate happiness comes when you are able to move at will between the physical and spiritual worlds as a Co-worker with God.

This is your destiny; this is your mission.

The Spiritual Laws of Life

*T*he odyssey of Soul teaches us to attune to the laws of life. It takes many lifetimes of bumps and bruises before all the lessons of life sink in. And when they do, we are granted the grace to partake consciously of the highest aspects of sainthood.

These laws speak to the heart, for they tell of the relationship between God and Soul. The supreme law is love. It gives each person an answer to the ancient riddle of life: What is my purpose here?

All Souls are moving into a greater circle of light and understanding.

Spiritual enlightenment and illumination come as we have contact with the Light and Sound of God. Sing *HU*, and you will find the Light and Sound within you.

Connecting Diamonds

*E*very event in our life is part of a divine plan that accounts for each so-called mistake or happening of chance. Life connects. Events in our lives are like diamonds. Invisible lines connect them in every possible direction and combination of points.

They lead over holy ground. It is there that the Holy Spirit does the wonders that help an individual do what he cannot do alone. It shields him. Its love and mercy are the grace that puts joy and goodness into everyday life.

Do you want to be happy? Then set out to learn about the connecting diamonds in your own life. They shimmer and glisten all around you.

Begin your search by singing *HU* as a love song to God for the strongest connection of all—your love bond with the Holy Spirit.

HELP IN DAILY LIFE

HU brings the strength
and wisdom to meet life

Soul Rises

As you chant the name of God, with love, for twenty minutes a day, the bindings that constrain Soul will begin to unwind. Not all at once, but very slowly, at a rate you can understand and accept.

As these bindings are released, Soul rises in spiritual freedom.

Ups and Downs

*L*ife goes up and down. We have times when everything is going our way, but there are also times when we're at the bottom. If we keep ourselves open to Spirit, there will be an equal balance.

When our fortunes hit bottom, we surrender to Spirit. Then we can go back up more naturally, and we'll maintain this rhythm of life. As life goes on around us, the detached state is that which runs right through the center; we are the balanced individual working in the Soul consciousness.

Singing *HU* can help you align with this natural, holy rhythm of life.

A Higher State

*I*f you want to lift yourself to a higher state of consciousness—so that the political issues, the family issues, the social issues of the day do not throw you out of balance, so that you can find a happier, more contented life while you're living here—sing *HU*, the most beautiful prayer.

The Strength to Meet Life

Sing *HU* once or twice a day for ten or fifteen minutes to spiritualize your state of consciousness.

During the time you're singing *HU*, you are saying to Divine Spirit, "I've opened myself to you. Give me the understanding and the wisdom to meet the waves of life, and the problems, troubles, and whatever else. Give me the strength to meet life."

Blessings

*H*U, this ancient name for God, is a love song to God. In singing it or holding it in your mind during times of need, it becomes a prayer of the highest sort.

It becomes a nondirected prayer. This means that we invite the Holy Spirit to take care of the affairs in our life according to the divine plan.

There is power and love in the word *HU*. It's another way of saying, "May the blessings be."

The Most Beautiful Prayer

Singing *HU*, the most beautiful prayer, is a spiritual technique you can use to keep your balance in this world. It can help you keep your perspective.

HU can protect. HU can give love, HU can heal. It can give peace of mind.

But don't expect HU to work as you want, because God's love, as it comes down and heals, does things its way. You have to have confidence and love in your heart. Sing *HU*, and a door will open.

Creators of Our World

*S*oul exists because God loves It.

You are Soul. In Its pure form, nothing is more elegant or regal than Soul, for It is the handiwork of the Creator.

Yet life is a mystery until we begin to understand that we can be the creators of our own world. In truth, what we are today is a creation of that which we have made from the past. There is a way to change the future.

Sing *HU*, this ancient name for God. Open yourself to the guidance, insights, love, and wonder of Divine Spirit raining Its blessings into your life. Silently say, "Thy will be done" with all your trust and gratitude.

The Power of God

*H*U is a name for God. Sing it to yourself, but first fill your heart with love.

When you're having any kind of trouble and you want an insight into what you can do or an understanding to get through the problem, sing the song of HU.

It has the power of God, and it has the love of God.

Highest Good

*W*hen you sing *HU*, you are spiritualizing your attention. You are saying, "I am putting all my attention, heart, and Soul upon the highest good I can imagine."

Finding Truth

*T*imes to chant *HU* include when you are in trouble. When things are not going well at the office, when you've had a bad day or someone else is having a bad day and you happen to be lower on the pecking order, you might sing *HU*.

It's a love song to God, a connection between Soul and the Divine Being, the Ancient of Days. If you really care about finding truth, sing *HU*.

Back in Line

*W*hen your day is hard, remember to sing *HU*. It puts you back in line with the Holy Spirit.

In All Ways

*I*f times are hard for you during the day, try to spiritualize yourself by singing *HU*. But sing it with love for God. This will lift you and help you through. It will make you a better person, in all ways and in all places, for all beings.

The Next Step

*H*U is an old name for God, and if you sing it, it's a love song to God. It's a very simple song, but if you're in trouble, in pain, in need of comfort, or in need of love, sing *HU* quietly to yourself.

If you know how to sing *HU*, you can open yourself to the Holy Spirit. You can open yourself to the help that It's offering you to help you take the next step.

A Higher Perspective

*H*U is a carrier of love between you and God.

HU can be sung silently at work, home, or anytime you feel a need to tune in to a higher perspective on your life. You might try experimenting with it when you face a challenging situation or want to open yourself to a more loving attitude.

Singing *HU* each day can lead to a deeper understanding of yourself and why things happen the way they do in your life. It opens your awareness to new viewpoints and attitudes. Anyone can work with the HU regardless of age, background, or religion.

HU, the most beautiful prayer, is a gift to the world.

Letting God Speak

*W*e know that when we make a clear, direct connection with the Holy Spirit, we will understand how It works in our life without even asking. It doesn't matter whether you pray or not, to God or anyone else—life brings you what you need, anyway.

The difference is, when you sing *HU* and sit silently in contemplation, you are letting God speak to you, to show you why certain things are going on in your life. In other words, you gain a greater understanding of the ways of the Holy Spirit.

The Silver Lining

*T*here's an old saying that every cloud has a silver lining. When a cloud comes into your life, look for the silver lining because it's there. If you can't see what the silver lining in the cloud is, sing *HU*. This will open your heart so you can say, "Thy will be done."

This is the real meaning of the word *HU*. It's adopting the attitude "Not my will, but thy will."

If you pray to God, be thankful for the gift of life. Thank God for that, then go on and handle the rest of your life as best you can.

UPLIFTMENT

Live your life as if you are one with the HU

Open Your Wings

*H*U is a love song to God that we sing. And it's to open your heart—like opening your wings. Opening your wings simply means opening your state of consciousness.

Like an Arrow Point

The Shariyat-Ki-Sugmad, Way of the Eternal, gives this golden wisdom on the sound of HU from the ECK Master Rebazar Tarzs:

" 'Let your faith, your inner trust and confidence stream forth; remove your inner obstacles and open yourself to truth.' It is this kind of faith, or inner awareness and open-mindedness, which finds its spontaneous expression, its liberation from an overwhelming psychic pressure, in the sacred sound of the HU. In this mantric sound all the positive and forward-pressing forces of the human, which are trying to blow up its limitations and burst the fetters of ignorance, are united and concentrated on the ECK, like an arrow point."

A Precious Gift

*I*n all heaven and earth no name is mightier than HU. It can lift the grieving heart to a temple of solace. A companion in trouble, it is likewise a friend in times of prosperity. And is it any wonder, for HU is Soul's most precious gift from God.

Upliftment for All

Sing *HU* softly, gently. Once among the most secret names of God, the Order of Vairagi Adepts has now brought it into the world for the upliftment of all. It is for those who desire true love, true freedom, wisdom, and truth.

In time, people everywhere will have the chance to sing this age-old, universal name for God. This is a new cycle in the spiritual history of the human community.

It will all be due to HU.

Key to Secret Worlds

You can open yourself and gain a greater awareness of who and what you are as Soul. You can do this by singing *HU*. Sing it to yourself, or sing it out loud. But do it every day.

HU is your key to your secret worlds. Once you learn to use this key, you will find a blending of your inner and outer worlds. You'll find yourself filling with love.

Looking for God

*W*hen you look for God-Realization, it must be something that lives within your heart in a gentle way. You know that no matter what happens on the spiritual path, it is always to lead you closer to the heart of God.

Let the song of HU be your compass on the journey. Day and night it leads you to your goal of spiritual freedom.

Attunement

*S*inging *HU* has been practiced for thousands of years in one form or another for inner attunement. In the same way a musician can use a tuning fork to find the right pitch, the person singing *HU* tunes in to a higher spiritual awareness.

HU is a carrier of love between you and God.

Purifying the Thought Stream

*T*here is a stream of consciousness from the mind that constantly goes through you. Chanting the HU keeps the stream pure.

Singing this sacred prayer song, this ancient name of God, purifies the thoughts which lead to your actions. It makes for a happier, more harmonious life.

You'll find by practicing this spiritual exercise every day upliftment comes as you are ready for it.

Communication from God

Sing the word *HU*. Sing it every day.

If you are ready, in a very short time you will have some definite recognition of a change for the better in your spiritual life.

There will be some kind of communication from God, directly or indirectly, that will bring upliftment to your life that was never there before.

Spiritual Grace

*E*verything in the right amount brings an abundance of life and fulfillment.

Nature reflects the laws of ECK. Therefore, observe its workings in the habits of birds, the cycles of plants, and the instincts of the reptiles and mammals.

All sing the glory of ECK; all teach the secrets of life.

Watch the coming and going of clouds, the waxing and waning of the moon, and the rising and setting of the sun. They reveal the natural order of creation.

Everything is right when there is neither too much nor too little for the time and place. So is it also with your spiritual life.

Eat foods that are good for you, because they build and restore the temple where Soul resides. Accept your emotions. Permit your mind to study, explore, and grow. Give yourself time for rest and contemplation. Love God.

(continued)

58

Give thanks for life, for it blesses you with revelations.

Life gives and takes, but always gives again. Be thankful for wisdom, be grateful for existence.

Life is precious. Love it, and it will return unfoldment to you a thousand times. We live in a time of unequaled spiritual opportunity.

This world and the things in it are for exploration, study, and joy.

Immerse yourself in living. Pet a cat, hug a child, or love a dog. Eat an ice-cream cone, have some pie—but do all things in moderation.

Ask yourself, What is for my highest good?

Take a walk by yourself or with a loved one. Listen for the Voice of God in the sounds of nature.

There is a plan to living; there is order. Love, and let God love you.

Relax and Restore

The mind can overreact to the rush of everyday living, leaving us on edge and out of sorts. We forget that help is as near as a few moments in contemplation.

At least once a day, let the Sound and Light of God enliven you with spiritual impulses. Gently chant *HU,* and the silent wind of God will enter the sacred temple of consciousness in the heart.

Once tensions relax, it is just moments until the healing current of Spirit begins to restore you.

Love's Golden Thread

The word is *HU*. It depends upon no human authority for validation. It is what it is.

From a practical standpoint, it is love's golden thread, drawing Soul closer to God, like an infant to its parent.

HU is a love song to God. It uplifts and purifies us of the evils that make life too much to bear. It heals our wounds, soothes our brow: sweet, but mighty, name of God.

Being the HU

You are a living spiritual exercise.

Every moment of your life, you must be the HU. This is more than just chanting *HU*. This is being the HU.

The Sound must always be in your atoms. It must be with you when you're driving, when you're at work, when you're home eating a meal with your family. The HU and you must be one and the same.

And if you make yourself more and more one with the HU, you will find that life is a more joyful place.

One with the HU

Live your life as if you are one with the HU, so that every moment of your life is a spiritual exercise.

When you are talking to a stranger, when you are with your loved ones, you are a spiritual exercise.

You are living and moving in the body of Divine Spirit.

$\mathscr{T}$HE LIGHT AND SOUND

HU opens your heart to God's Voice

The Highest Form of Love

*T*he Light and Sound of God are the two aspects of the Holy Spirit that equal divine love.

The highest form of love that you can bring into your life is through the Light and Sound. That's what we look for.

Let Spirit Take Charge

*T*he Sound of God is contained in the word *HU*, a secret or sacred name for the SUGMAD.

This word can be used quietly at work, at home, or anytime you face a crisis. After you have done everything you can do, you sing this word quietly, and then stand back and let Spirit take charge.

The Language of Life

*H*U is woven into the language of life.

It is the Sound of all sounds. It is the wind in the leaves, falling rain, thunder of jets, singing of birds, the awful rumble of a tornado.

Again, Its sound is heard in laughter, weeping, the din of city traffic, ocean waves, and the quiet rippling of a mountain stream.

HU is both a name for God and a sound of the Audible Life Stream, which we know as the ECK, or Holy Spirit.

HU is a charged name for God that can spiritually uplift the people of any religion.

Joy and Wonder

*H*ere's a spiritual exercise to try if you want to experience the Light or Sound of God:

Shut your eyes and look into the Spiritual Eye. (It's between your eyebrows, in the center of your forehead.) Sing *HU*, an ancient name for God, one of the most powerful words for spiritual upliftment.

As you sing *HU*, listen for a holy Sound. It may come in any number of ways: like the sound of a rumbling train, a singing bird, buzzing bees, a mellow flute, or even soothing guitars.

It brings joy and wonder.

The holy sounds are the creative action of the Life Force, the ECK, as It moves atoms in the invisible worlds. The Sound to reach your ears resonates with your state of consciousness.

While singing *HU*, imagine the holy Sound of God cascading over you, like a waterfall of sparkling pure waters. It is cleansing the blemishes of spirit.

(continued)

The Sound opens a secret path to the joys of love and grace. You find peace, joy, and spiritual freedom.

The Returning Wave

An aspect of Spirit, even more important than the Light, is the Sound.

The Sound Current is actually the Voice of God. This Voice, the creative current from God, is like a pebble thrown into a quiet lake, causing ripples to go out. These waves must always come back to the center; it's the returning wave that we seek.

This is what Soul is looking for: to return to the God center, the God Consciousness.

Look for this wave. Listen for this sound as you sing the sacred *HU*.

The Voice of God

*W*hat are the Sound and Light of God? What do they signify?

The Light and Sound are the Voice of God, the expression of God's love for us. They comprise the whole of God's love. Together, they are what religion calls the Holy Spirit.

In speaking of the Light, we say, "Yes, there is such a thing as the Light of God. It's a thousand times brighter than any sun, or it may be softer than the light of a golden moon."

The Light of God illumines your entire being, inside and out.

Sounds of God on the inner planes may be like the musical instruments, birds, choirs, machines, the ocean, high-pitched whistles, a murmur or crescendo of wind or water. Maybe the tinkling of joyous laughter. All these are holy sounds.

A word to help open your heart to God's

(continued)

love is *HU*. It is an ancient, sacred name for God.

Sing it with love as you look and listen within.

Holy Alliance

*A*nytime you sing *HU* as a love offering to the Lord of all creation, your heart fills with the Light and Sound of God. They are the twin aspects of ECK, the Holy Spirit.

HU, the name of God, brings us into a holy alliance with the Light and Sound, the Word of God. Should the worlds tremble and all else fail, HU carries us into the ocean of God's love and mercy.

Approaching the Altar

*T*he Sound and Light carry out God's scheme of creation. So the highest anyone can aspire to is a life of high creativity, but always guided by the force of divine love.

This is how to be most like God.

Try this simple spiritual exercise to help you hear and see the two aspects of God, the Light and Sound.

Put your attention on your Spiritual Eye, a point just above and behind your eyebrows. With eyes lightly shut, begin to sing *HU*. But fill your heart with love before you approach the altar of God, because only the pure may come.

Be patient. God speaks only when you are able to listen.

Your Love Song

*T*he best way to make contact with the Light and Sound of God is through the Spiritual Exercises of ECK.

One of these is simply to sing *HU,* a name for God. This is your love song to God, to be sung in your own way, in your own unique style.

Embodied in that one word are all the sounds of creation: the singing of birds, crickets, frogs, and other sounds of nature, the symphonies, chamber music, and operas of Mozart, the country-western music, and more.

The nearest you can come to hearing the Voice of God, and therefore following the will of God and finding the love of God, is through the Sound Current, the sound of HU.

Making a Connection

*W*e want to make a connection between ourselves here on earth and God above, however you see this.

A way to do this is with the sound of HU. HU is another name for God and opens your heart to the Light and Sound.

The connection is so natural. Sing *HU* every day, and invite this love into your heart and being.

Rhythm of Life

You can find the path to love, wisdom, and spiritual freedom by singing *HU* every day, until HU becomes a part of you and you of it.

You will begin to vibrate in tune with the Sound Current. Once you enter the rhythm of life, you *become* the Song of HU itself.

Love the Song of HU

*T*he Spiritual Exercises of ECK are a key to your secret worlds.

They can be so simple. Just close your eyes in some quiet place, and sing *HU* to yourself. Relax, and let the love of God into your heart.

When you do the spiritual exercises, you set aside a time to be quiet and open yourself to the Holy Spirit, the Light and Sound of God. You will come to see and live your life more fully.

You will come to love the song of HU.

A World of Golden Light

*O*ccasionally we go to a far world which has a beauty beyond words. There is no true way to describe what is seen. The closest is to say it's a world illuminated by two golden suns, and everything is seen through a golden veil. When Soul comes here and begins walking into the land of gold, It wants never to return; It wants to go on forever.

There is a yearning to go even farther, farther than ever before, because the love of God always draws you on.

But our responsibilities bring us back. And the only way we can ever go further into the heart of God is to face our responsibilities to serve God in this world. This is the paradox that both allows us to grow and gives us the yearning to want to grow.

Sing *HU*, and you will find the way to the world of Golden Light that is exactly right for you.

About the Author

 Author Harold Klemp is known as a pioneer of today's focus on "everyday spirituality." He was raised on a Wisconsin farm and attended divinity school. He also served in the US Air Force.

In 1981, after lifetimes of training, he became the spiritual leader of Eckankar, the Path of Spiritual Freedom. His full title is Sri Harold Klemp, the Mahanta, the Living ECK Master. His mission is to help people find their way back to God in this life.

Each year, Harold Klemp speaks to thousands of seekers at Eckankar seminars. Author of more than one hundred books, he continues to write, including many articles and spiritual-study discourses. His inspiring and practical approach to spirituality helps many thousands of people worldwide find greater freedom, wisdom, and love in their lives.

Advanced Spiritual Living

Go higher, further, deeper with your spiritual exploration!

ECK membership brings many unique benefits and a focus on the ECK discourses.

These are dynamic spiritual courses you study at home, one per month.

The first year of study brings *The Easy Way Discourses* by Harold Klemp, with uplifting spiritual exercises, audio excerpts from his seminar talks, and activities to personalize your spiritual journey. Classes are available in many areas.

Each year you choose to continue with ECK membership can bring new levels of divine freedom, inner strength to meet the challenges of life, and direct experience with the love and power of God.

Here's a sampling of titles from *The Easy Way Discourses:*

- In Soul You Are Free

- Reincarnation—Why You Came to Earth Again
- The Master Principle
- The God Worlds—Where No One Has Gone Before?

How to Get Started

For free books and more information about Eckankar:

- Visit www.Eckankar.org;
- Call 1-800-LOVE GOD (1-800-568-3463) (USA and Canada only); or
- Write to: ECKANKAR, Dept. BK 131, PO Box 2000, Chanhassen, MN 55317-2000 USA.

To order Eckankar books online, you can visit www.ECKBooks.org.

To receive your advanced spiritual-study discourses, along with other annual membership benefits, go to www.Eckankar.org (click on "Membership" then "Online Membership Application"). You can also call Eckankar at (952) 380-2222 to apply. Or write to the address above, Att: Membership.

For Further Reading and Study

HU, the Most Beautiful Prayer
Harold Klemp

Singing *HU*, the ancient name for God, can open your heart and lead you to a new understanding of yourself. Includes a CD of the HU Song.

HU: A Love Song to God
(available on CD)

This recording carries highlights of Sri Harold Klemp's talks on the HU, as well as spiritual exercises that bring the Light and Sound of God into the life of the seeker. It includes a twenty-minute HU song with thousands of people singing this powerful, majestic love song to God.

Book 17

The Mahanta Transcripts Series
Harold Klemp

The Mahanta Transcripts, books 1–17, are from Harold Klemp's talks at Eckankar seminars. He has taught thousands how to have a natural, direct relationship with the Holy Spirit. The stories and wonderful insights contained in these talks will lead you to deeper spiritual understanding.

84

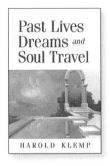

Past Lives, Dreams, and Soul Travel
Harold Klemp

These stories and exercises help you find your true purpose, discover greater love than you've ever known, and learn that spiritual freedom is within reach.

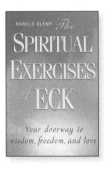

The Spiritual Exercises of ECK
Harold Klemp

This book is a staircase with 131 steps leading to the doorway to spiritual freedom, self-mastery, wisdom, and love. A comprehensive volume of spiritual exercises for every need.

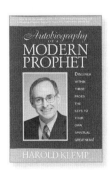

Autobiography of a Modern Prophet
Harold Klemp

This riveting story of Harold Klemp's climb up the Mountain of God will help you discover the keys to your own spiritual greatness.

Glossary

Words set in SMALL CAPS are defined elsewhere in this glossary.

Blue Light How the MAHANTA often appears in the inner worlds to the chela or seeker.

ECK The Life Force, the Holy Spirit, or Audible Life Current which sustains all life.

Eckankar *EHK-ahn-kahr* The Path of Spiritual Freedom. Also known as the Ancient Science of SOUL TRAVEL. A truly spiritual way of life for the individual in modern times. The teachings provide a framework for anyone to explore their own spiritual experiences. Established by PAUL TWITCHELL, the modern-day founder, in 1965. The word means Co-worker with God.

ECK Masters Spiritual Masters who can assist and protect people in their spiritual studies and travels. The ECK Masters are from a long line of God-Realized SOULS who know the responsibility that goes with spiritual freedom.

God-Realization The state of God Consciousness. Complete and conscious awareness of God.

HU *HYOO* The most ancient, secret name for God. The singing of the word *HU* is considered a love song to God. It can be sung aloud or silently to oneself to align with God's love.

Klemp, Harold The present MAHANTA, the LIVING ECK MASTER. SRI Harold Klemp became the Mahanta, the Living ECK Master in 1981. His spiritual name is WAH Z.

Living ECK Master The title of the spiritual leader of ECKANKAR. He leads SOUL back to God. He teaches in the physical world as the Outer Master, in the dream state as

86

Glossary

the Dream Master, and in the spiritual worlds as the Inner Master. SRI HAROLD KLEMP became the MAHANTA, the Living ECK Master in 1981.

Mahanta An expression of the Spirit of God that is always with you. Sometimes seen as a BLUE LIGHT or Blue Star or in the form of the Mahanta, the LIVING ECK MASTER. The highest state of God Consciousness on earth, only embodied in the Living ECK Master. He is the Living Word.

planes Levels of existence, such as the Physical, Astral, Causal, Mental, Etheric, and SOUL Planes.

Rebazar Tarzs A Tibetan ECK MASTER known as the Torchbearer of ECKANKAR in the lower worlds.

Self-Realization SOUL recognition. The entering of Soul into the Soul PLANE and there beholding Itself as pure Spirit. A state of seeing, knowing, and being.

Shariyat-Ki-Sugmad The sacred scriptures of ECKANKAR. The scriptures are comprised of twelve volumes in the spiritual worlds. The first two were transcribed from the inner PLANES by PAUL TWITCHELL, modern-day founder of Eckankar.

Soul The True Self, an individual, eternal spark of God. The inner, most sacred part of each person. Soul can see, know, and perceive all things. It is the creative center of Its own world.

Soul Travel The expansion of consciousness. The ability of SOUL to transcend the physical body and travel into the spiritual worlds of God. Soul Travel is taught only by the LIVING ECK MASTER. It helps people unfold spiritually and can provide proof of the existence of God and life after death.

Sound and Light of ECK The Holy Spirit. The two aspects through which God appears in the lower worlds. People can experience them by looking and listening within themselves and through SOUL TRAVEL.

Glossary

Spiritual Exercises of ECK   Daily practices for direct, personal experiences with the Sound Current. Creative techniques using contemplation and the singing of sacred words to bring the higher awareness of Soul into daily life.

Sri *SREE*   A title of spiritual respect, similar to reverend or pastor, used for those who have attained the Kingdom of God. In Eckankar, it is reserved for the Mahanta, the Living ECK Master.

Sugmad *SOOG-mahd*   A sacred name for God. It is the source of all life, neither male nor female, the Ocean of Love and Mercy.

Twitchell, Paul   An American ECK Master who brought the modern teachings of Eckankar to the world through his writings and lectures. His spiritual name is Peddar Zaskq.

Wah Z *WAH zee*   The spiritual name of Sri Harold Klemp. It means the secret doctrine. It is his name in the spiritual worlds.

For more explanations of Eckankar terms, see *A Cosmic Sea of Words: The ECKANKAR Lexicon* by Harold Klemp.